Cocktails

100 Classic Cocktails

by Barry Shelby

A TINY FOLIO™

ABBEVILLE PRESS   PUBLISHERS

NEW YORK   LONDON

Contents

Introduction

At a tiny, dark bar named The Angel's Share in lower Manhattan, young bartenders mix drinks with exquisite care, agitating stainless steel shakers, held slightly above one shoulder, their movements precise. It is a dance.

Across town at Bar d'O, low-slung couches are filled with convivial, thirsty patrons as a dj spins Sergio Mendez or some other piece of space-age bachelor pad music, the tasteful (if camp) soundtrack for the lounge scene.

And on the opposite coast, in Los Angeles, the fifties-inflected Dresden Room features the vocal and piano stylings of Marty and Elayne, as middle-aged bartenders in white shirts and black bow ties look as if they have been slinging libations for more than thirty years. The place is rarely less than packed.

On the Internet one can find the Virtual Bar, a web site devoted to drink mixing, lacking only conversational din and secondhand smoke. The electronic version of *Wired* magazine has offered a cocktail of the week via e-mail. The 1997 sleeper movie hit *Swingers* epitomized the rise of a new cocktail nation—albeit a young, male-dominated one.

Increasingly, invitations are extended to come over for cocktails—which generally means the guests are in by 7:30 P.M. and out no later than nine, leaving the hosts free to entertain their own interests.

The cocktail is making a comeback.

There is something sumptuous, decadent, urbane, about the cocktail and the cocktail hour. There is something nostalgic about it, too. Its heyday now seems a time when life was easier, fun, at times classier and less inhibited. But have we really revived the cocktail age and returned to the glory days of the 1920s and '30s, the apex of cocktail popularity?

Writer Diana Trilling, recalling her courtship with liberal intellectual Lionel Trilling in 1929, said: "Neither of us was entirely sober when we were together." Their romance was lubricated with Brandy Alexanders and Bullfrogs. The cocktail age coincided with Prohibition, and not by accident. Demon alcohol could be mixed with—and disguised by—more innocent ingredients.

By all accounts, this was only a U.S. phenomenon initially, but it did not take long to spread overseas. British author Andrew Barr writes in *Drink*, "Cocktails became all the rage among young people in the early 1920s because they were

regarded as new and American, and because by drinking cocktails they were able to outrage their elders." But by the end of the decade, the practice could no longer offend. Drinks prior to dinner had replaced postprandial cordials—for everyone.

The English writer Alec Waugh claimed in 1924 to have created the cocktail party, having invited guests over for tea and instead served them a rum punch mixed by a friend visiting from New York. Barr says that there were two very practical reasons for the popularity of cocktail parties: they were cheaper and easier than inviting people to dinner.

But the cocktail certainly did not originate in the Roaring Twenties. Alcoholic drinks were being mixed as early as the fourteenth century, when ale was combined with mead (fermented honey and water) and called a Bragget. The Mint Julep is believed to have been first made in eighteenth-century Virginia, when mint sprigs were put in rum or brandy and served as morning eye-openers. Victorians knew about cocktails, imbibing Gum Ticklers and Corpse Revivers (a version of which is still served today). And Charles Dickens wrote fondly of rum punches and the characters who mixed them.

As for partaking in the afternoon or early evening, the French began drinking aperitifs—before-dinner drinks (though probably not mixed ones)—around the time of the

Revolution, although the practice was not widespread until a century later. Some believe that the advent of World War I is what popularized the aperitif. Nerves were frazzled and an early drink, if not several, was in order.

During the golden age, the demand for new and more exotic mixed drinks grew, and bartenders complied. At Harry's American Bar in Paris, the Sidecar and White Lady were created. The Mimosa is credited to bartenders at the Ritz in London.

Following in the wake of the cocktail era came Victor "Trader Vic" Bergeron, the San Francisco restaurateur, and his mixture of lime, curaçao, and rum in the 1940s: the Mai Tai. In the 1950s the Screwdriver was invented, supposedly by American oil riggers working the Middle East. They combined vodka and orange juice, and stirred the drink with the only implement at hand.

New drinks continue to be devised. As a basic restaurant and beverage guide warns about the cocktail: "This is the exotic section of the drinks market. . . . It is essential that bar staff keep themselves up-to-date and conversant with modern trends."

But if requests for the latest concoctions can confound, no less confusing is the etymology of "cocktail." The word is of mysterious provenance. According to the *Bloomsbury Dictionary of Word Origins,* "It first appeared (in America) in the first decade of the 19th century, . . . meaning horse with a cocked tail—that is, one cut short and so made to stick up like a cock's tail—but whether the two words are connected, and if so, how the drink came to be named after such a horse, [is] not at all clear."

French officers in George Washington's army were said to favor a mixed drink called a Coquetel. After the Revolution, a barmaid named Betsy Flanagan (the widow of a revolutionary officer) at Hall's Corner Tavern in New York decorated glasses with the tails of roosters that she allegedly stole from a neighbor. One night an inebriated customer slurred his request: give me a glass of those cock tails—or so the story goes.

Then again, perhaps it is true that rooster tails were used to stir the drinks served to gamblers on the Mississippi. One more tale from the South has a pharmacist in New Orleans giving a restorative mixed drink to customers during cold spells. He served it in an egg cup—or coquetier. And Mexico gets a share of credit, too. In one version, locals drank a mixture of something that was stirred with a root known as cola de gallo, or cock's tail. In a more romantic vein, an alluring young Mexican woman named Coctel gains fame for her mixed drinks.

The first use of the word in print has been attributed to a newspaper in Hudson, New York, which in 1806 described the cocktail as "a stimulating liquor composed of spirits of any kind, sugar, water, and bitters." American barman Jerry Thomas produced the first book of cocktail recipes in the 1860s. Hundreds were to follow, offering ideas to the adventurous barkeep and to those wishing to play the host at home. Enter the aspiring home entertainer.

The cocktail party is a particular cultural institution. It is not only meant to gather friends but is often an occasion when mere acquaintances and even strangers are thrown together. Given the early hour associated with it, appetizers are frequently included, thus making it, in the eyes of a sociologist, a drinking and eating ritual that reduces barriers between people. If drinking customs are not fixed (or at least vary widely), there is nevertheless a standard of behavior when it comes to the cocktail party. One is expected to drink heavily but never behave boorishly.

The ritual's origins can be traced to the ancient Greek symposium, at which men gathered for an evening of talk, entertainment—and drink, which had a significant (if historically downplayed) place in Greek culture. Thomas Babor writes in *Alcohol: Customs and Rituals,* "The evening . . . invariably ended with drunkenness." The contemporary equivalent is the cocktail party, which stands in contrast to the beer-kegger, the twentieth century's take on the symposium's successor—the Roman Bacchanalia.

The customs of the cocktail often obey regional and seasonal prescriptions, as well. The Mint Julep has long been associated with the Kentucky Derby, and rounds of the beverage are hoisted every night before the race. For purists, serving a Hot Toddy in August is about as absurd as offering a Seabreeze on the dark days of winter. Holden Caulfield remarked on such a faux pas in *The Catcher in the Rye:* "She and old Marty were drinking Tom Collinses—in the middle of December for God's sake. They didn't know any better."

The one hundred mixed drinks in this volume were carefully chosen from various compendiums of contemporary cocktails, which include recipes that number in the thousands.

First and foremost, they are classics. Don't expect to find the Fuzzy Navel or Sex on the Beach or any other such concoctions. For while it is surely true that no one can predict the drinking fads of the future, over the past eighty years or so, from the cocktail age of the twenties to its present revival, a track record has been established for the tried and true.

Thus the Rusty Nail, however recondite, belongs nonetheless in the cocktail canon.

Many of the drinks here—for instance, the Tequila Sunrise—carry a visual esthetic that makes them as pleasant to regard as to drink. Others, like the Kamikaze and the Stinger, are notorious for their potency. A few notably cover the taste of alcohol with great success—the Madras and Cosmopolitan, for example. Some have evocative names: Golden Cadillac and Zombie. They beg to be served occasionally, if only to slake one's curiosity. A couple are not classic cocktails per se, but Planter's Punch and Egg Nog belong in any home bartender's repertoire.

My interest in bartending may not be much different from yours: I'm an amateur, a lover of the art and ritual of mixing drinks, who takes great pleasure in having friends and family—or perfect strangers—enjoy them. The real secret to successful bartending is understanding not only the amounts and proportions but the process. A bad Martini will result if all one does is add a half teaspoon of dry vermouth to an ounce and a half of gin or vodka.

But to make an excellent Martini is not terribly difficult either. The chilling of the glass and the subtle shaking (or stirring) of the concoction just before serving, however, are indispensable. And never, ever, chill your spirits in advance: it alters their consistency.

Attitude and care are what's important, a point not lost on Dickens, who wrote in *Our Mutual Friend*, "However particular you may be in allotting your materials, so much will depend upon the individual gifts, and there being a feeling thrown into it."

Finally, the popularity of the cocktail continues today for many of the same reasons of yesteryear. Because temperance movements have not lost their influence, a drink downed before sunset remains a form of rebellion, however mild. For some, the cocktail is a way of enjoying the effects of strong liquor without having to choke it down straight, no chaser. (It should be said that some purists feel the cocktail is an abomination—akin to mixing Chardonnay and Burgundy.) And there is of course the communal, convivial aspect of the cocktail hour, even if we have long dispensed with the habit, from the days of the Bragget, of passing around the same glass. The need to see and speak with people—whether to broaden horizons or establish business contacts—will always need sating. A drink helps ease our way.

So, here's to the reborn cocktail community . . . and to your health. Cheers!

100
Drink
Recipes

Americano

2 oz. sweet vermouth
2 oz. Campari
club soda
lemon

Pour sweet vermouth and Campari into
a highball glass, over ice cubes. Fill
with club soda and stir. Add a twist of
lemon peel or garnish with wedge.

Banana Daiquiri

1½ oz. light rum
1 tbsp. triple sec
1½ oz. lime juice
1 tsp. sugar
1 medium banana, sliced
stemmed cherry

Combine ingredients in a blender with
1 cup crushed ice and blend until
smooth. Pour into a wineglass (or any
other stemmed glass). Garnish with a
cherry. *See* Daiquiri.

$\mathcal{B}$ & $\mathcal{B}$

½ oz. Benedictine
1 oz. brandy

Mix ingredients in an old-fashioned
glass with ice.

Beachcomber

1 ½ oz. light rum
½ oz. triple sec
½ oz. lime juice
1 dash maraschino liqueur
lime

Shake all ingredients with ice and
strain into a chilled cocktail glass with a
sugared rim. Garnish with a lime
wheel.

Bellini

3 oz. pureed peaches (or peach nectar)
1 dash lemon juice
3 oz. chilled champagne (dry)
1 dash black currant juice or grenadine

Pour white peach juice into a wine
glass or champagne flute, if available.
Add a dash of lemon juice (more if
peach nectar is substituted) and a dash
of black currant juice or grenadine for
color. Fill with chilled champagne.

Bitters Highball

dashes bitters
ginger ale or club soda

Fill a highball glass with bitters, ice
cubes, and ginger ale or club soda.
Add a twist of lemon peel, if desired,
and stir.

Blackjack

1 oz. kirschwasser
½ oz. brandy
1 oz. coffee

Shake all ingredients with cracked ice
and strain into an old-fashioned glass,
over ice cubes.

Black Russian

1½ oz. vodka
¾ oz. coffee liqueur

Pour both ingredients over ice cubes
into an old-fashioned glass and stir.

Bloody Mary

1½ oz. vodka
4 oz. tomato juice
1 dash lemon juice
½ tsp. Worcestershire sauce
2–3 drops Tabasco sauce
celery stalk
salt and pepper to taste

Shake all ingredients with ice and strain
into a highball glass over ice cubes. Add
a wedge of lime and celery stalk. Try a
dash or two of cayenne pepper, a
teaspoon or so of horseradish, or a
pepper-infused vodka for a bit more bite.

Bourbon Highball

2 oz. bourbon
ginger ale, club soda, or tap water
lemon

Fill a highball glass with bourbon,
mixer of choice, and ice cubes. Add
twist of lemon peel, if desired, and stir.

*"I can offer you port, brandy,
Madeira or Tia Maria."*

*"Hmm, sounds nice.
How about a cocktail of all
four? Let's live dangerously."*

—FROM *COMING TO TERMS*,
IMOGEN WINN

Brandy Alexander

½ oz. crème de cacao (brown)
¾ oz. brandy
½ oz. heavy cream

Shake all ingredients well with cracked
ice and strain into a cocktail glass.
Nutmeg is an optional garnish.

Brandy Flip

2 oz. brandy
¾ oz. cream
1 tsp. powdered sugar
1 egg yolk
nutmeg

Combine all ingredients well with ice cubes in a shaker. Strain into a cocktail glass and garnish with nutmeg sprinkles. The classic flip does not include cream; it can be left out, if desired.

Bronx

1½ oz. gin
½ oz. dry vermouth
½ oz. sweet vermouth
juice of ½ orange

Shake with ice and strain into a cocktail glass. Serve with a slice of orange. For a dry Bronx, forego the sweet vermouth.

Caipirinha

2 tsp. granulated sugar
1 lime, cut into 8 wedges
2 ½ oz. cachaça

Mash the lime and sugar in an old-fashioned glass. Pour the cachaça into the glass and stir well. Fill the glass with ice cubes or crushed ice and stir again.

Campari Cocktail

1 oz. Campari
¾ oz. vodka
dash Angostura bitters
lemon

Shake well with ice in a shaker and
strain into a chilled cocktail glass.
Twist lemon peel over the drink before
dropping it into the glass.

Cape Codder

1½ oz. vodka
5 oz. cranberry juice
lime

Pour vodka and juice over ice in a
highball glass. Stir well. Garnish with a
wedge of lime.

Champagne Cocktail

1 cube sugar
2 dashes bitters
chilled champagne
lemon

Place sugar and bitters in a chilled
champagne flute and fill with
champagne. Add a twist of lemon peel.

Champagne Flip

1 egg yolk
½ tsp. powdered sugar
¼ oz. cream
dashes Cointreau
¾ oz. brandy
champagne
nutmeg

Shake first five ingredients well over ice
cubes in a shaker, strain into a
champagne flute, carefully fill with
champagne, and sprinkle the top with
nutmeg.

Chimayo Cocktail

1 ½ oz. tequila
½ oz. lime juice
½ oz. apple juice
apple

Shake all ingredients well with ice and
strain into old-fashioned glass with ice.
Garnish with apple wedge.

Corpse Reviver

¾ oz. sweet dark vermouth
¾ oz. Calvados (or applejack)
¾ oz. brandy

Stir well over ice cubes in a mixing
glass, strain into a cocktail glass, and
serve with a glass of ice water.

Cosmopolitan

1.5 oz. vodka
1 oz. triple sec
1 dash of cranberry juice (or to taste)

Shake with ice and strain into a chilled
cocktail glass.

Cuba Libre

juice of ½ lime
2 oz. light rum
cola

Put lime juice and twist of lime into
highball glass with ice cubes, and add
rum. Fill with cola.

Cynar Cocktail

1 oz. sweet light vermouth
1 oz. Cynar
orange

Pour vermouth and Cynar over ice
cubes in an old-fashioned glass, stir,
and squeeze orange wedge over drink
before dropping it into the glass.

Daiquiri

juice of 1 lime
1 tsp. powdered sugar
1½ oz. light rum

Shake with ice and strain into a cocktail glass.

Dubonnet Cocktail

1 ½ oz. Dubonnet Rouge
½ oz. gin
1 dash bitters
lemon

In a mixing glass half-filled with ice cubes, combine the Dubonnet, gin, and bitters. Stir well. Strain into a cocktail glass and garnish with the lemon twist.

Egg Nog

(*serves 8–10*)
1 dozen medium eggs
1 cup sugar
1½ quarts whole milk
1 pint heavy whipped cream
750 ml. (1 fifth) cognac

Separate eggs, and beat yolks in a large
serving bowl, adding sugar while
beating. Stir in milk and cream. Slowly
add cognac. Refrigerate for one hour.
Before serving, whip egg whites stiff,
and mix into nog. Dust with nutmeg
and serve in a large punch bowl.

Gibson

2 ½ oz. gin
1 ½ tsp. dry vermouth
3 cocktail onions

In a mixing glass half-filled with ice
cubes, combine the gin and vermouth.
Stir well. Strain into a cocktail glass.
Garnish with onions.

Gimlet

1 oz. lime juice
1½ oz. gin

Shake well with ice and strain into a
cocktail glass. Powdered sugar may be
added, to taste. *See also* Vodka Gimlet.

Gin & Bitters

See Pink Gin.

"The American colony is divided into three parts: those who have their cocktails at Lelands's or Doney's, a small sect who have them at home, and the third part, a tiny and suspect group, which does not have cocktails."

—FROM *WORLD SO WIDE*,
SINCLAIR LEWIS

Gin Fizz

juice of ½ lemon
1 tsp. powdered sugar
2 oz. gin
club soda

Shake first three ingredients with ice
and strain into highball glass with a few
ice cubes. Fill with club soda and stir.

Gin Rickey

1½ oz. gin
lime
club soda

Combine juice of half a lime and gin in
a highball glass with ice cubes. Fill with
club soda and stir. Garnish with a
wedge of lime before serving.

Gin & Tonic

2 oz. gin
tonic water
lime

Squeeze lime over ice cubes in a
highball glass, add gin, and fill with
tonic water. Stir.

Golden Cadillac

1 oz. Galliano
1 oz. crème de cacao (white)
1 oz. light cream

Combine ingredients with a half-cup of
crushed ice in blender at low speed for
ten seconds. Strain into a chilled
champagne flute or cocktail glass.
Another version of this drink can be
made by shaking all ingredients over
ice and then simply straining the drink
into a cocktail glass. Other variations
on the Golden Cadillac include orange
juice.

Golden Dream

1 tbsp. orange juice
½ oz. triple sec
1 oz. Galliano
1 tbsp. light cream

Shake all ingredients with ice and
strain into a cocktail glass.

Golden Fizz

1½ oz. gin
juice of ½ lemon
¼ oz. orange juice
1 tsp. powdered sugar
1 egg yolk
club soda

Combine gin, lemon juice, orange
juice, sugar, egg yolk, and ice in a
mixing glass and shake well. Strain into
highball glass, fill with soda, and add
lemon slice.

Grasshopper

½ oz. crème de menthe (green)
¾ oz. crème de cacao (white)
1 oz. light cream

Shake all ingredients with ice and
strain into a cocktail glass.

Greyhound

1½ oz. vodka
5 oz. grapefruit juice

Pour into highball glass over ice cubes.
Stir well.

Half & Half

See Vermouth Cocktail.

Harvey Wallbanger

1½ oz. vodka
4 oz. orange juice
½ oz. Galliano

Pour vodka and orange juice into a
highball glass filled with ice cubes. Stir.
Float Galliano on top.

Hot Toddy

1 cube sugar
boiling water
2 oz. blended whiskey
lemon
nutmeg

Put sugar into a heat-resistant glass and
fill two-thirds full with boiling water.
Add whiskey and stir. Decorate with a
slice of lemon and sprinkle with
nutmeg. Cinnamon sticks are an
optional garnish.

*"Whiskey doesn't sustain life,
but, whin taken hot with
wather, a lump iv sugar,
a piece iv lemon peel,
and just th' dustin' iv
the nutmeg-grater,
it makes life sustainable."*

—FROM *MR. DOOLEY'S PHILOSOPHY*,
FINLEY PETER DUNNE

Hurricane

1 oz. dark rum
1 oz. light rum
1 tbsp. passion fruit syrup
2 tsp. lime juice
lime

Shake all ingredients with ice and
strain into a highball glass over crushed
ice; garnish with a lime wedge. For a
fruitier Hurricane add equal parts
orange juice and pineapple juice, about
½ oz. each.

Imperial

1½ oz. dry vermouth
1½ oz. gin
½ tsp. cherry liqueur
1 dash bitters
cherry

Stir all ingredients with ice and strain
into a cocktail glass. Garnish with a
cherry.

Irish Coffee

1½ oz. Irish whiskey
hot coffee
whipped cream

Pour Irish whiskey into Irish coffee glass rimmed with sugar. Fill with coffee, leaving half an inch or so at the top of the glass. Cover surface to brim with whipped cream.

Kamikaze

½ oz. lime juice
½ oz. triple sec
1½ oz. vodka

Shake all ingredients with ice and
strain into a cocktail glass.

Kir

3 oz. white wine
1 splash crème de cassis
lemon

Pour wine over ice in an old-fashioned
glass. Add crème de cassis and a twist
of lemon, and stir. For a Kir Royale
(pictured), combine the crème de
cassis with 6 oz. of champagne and
serve in a wineglass or champagne
flute.

Knickerbocker

1 oz. gin
¾ oz. dry vermouth
dashes sweet light vermouth (or rosso)
lemon

Stir well in a mixing glass filled with
ice, strain into a chilled cocktail glass,
and squeeze lemon twist over the drink
before dropping it into the glass.

Long Island Iced Tea

½ oz. vodka
½ oz. gin
½ oz. light rum
½ oz. tequila
juice of ½ lemon
1 dash cola

Combine ingredients and pour over ice
into a highball glass. Add cola for
color. Garnish with slice of lemon.

Madras

1½ oz. vodka
4 oz. cranberry juice
1 oz. orange juice
lime

Pour all ingredients into a highball
glass over ice and stir. Garnish with a
wedge of lime.

Mai Tai

½ tsp. powdered sugar
2 oz. light rum
1 oz. triple sec
1 tbsp. orgeat (or almond-flavored syrup)
1 tbsp. grenadine
1 tbsp. lime juice
pineapple, cherry

Shake all ingredients with ice and strain
into an old-fashioned glass about one-
third full of crushed ice. Decorate with a
maraschino cherry speared to a wedge of
fresh pineapple. Serve with straws. For a
kickier Mai Tai, try topping the drink
with a dash of high-proof dark rum.

Manhattan

¾ oz. sweet vermouth
1½ oz. blended whiskey
stemmed cherry

Stir vermouth and whiskey with ice
and strain into a cocktail glass or mix
on the rocks in an old-fashioned glass.
Serve with a cherry. *See also* Rob Roy.

Margarita

1½ oz. tequila
½ oz. triple sec
1 oz. lemon or lime juice

Rub rim of a cocktail glass with the
lemon or lime rind and dip rim in salt.
Shake all ingredients with ice and
strain into the salt-rimmed glass.

*"I am prepared to believe
that a dry martini
slightly impairs the palate,
but think what it
does for the soul."*

—ALEC WAUGH

Martini

1½ oz. gin
½ tsp. dry vermouth

Stir vermouth and gin over ice cubes in mixing glass. Strain into chilled cocktail glass. Serve with a twist of lemon peel or olive, if desired. A sweet Martini can be made with equal parts gin and sweet vermouth. The "traditional" ratio is said to be two parts gin to one part dry vermouth, though this is far from the favored combination. *See also* Park Avenue.

"Dry Martinis
for everyone?
There is no better
tranquilizer."

—FROM *THE DISCREET CHARM*
OF THE BOURGEOISIE,
LUIS BUÑUEL

Melon Patch

1 oz. melon liqueur
½ oz. triple sec
½ oz. vodka
club soda
orange

Shake melon liqueur, vodka, and triple
sec well with ice, and pour into a
chilled cocktail glass. Fill with soda
and garnish with orange, or, for the
more enterprising, melon balls.

Metropolitan

1½ oz. vodka
½ oz. lime juice
¾ oz. cranberry juice
1 dash crème de cassis
lime

Shake all ingredients with ice and
strain into a cocktail glass. Squeeze
lime wedge over drink before dropping
into glass.

Mexican Coffee

1 oz. coffee liqueur
½ oz. tequila
5 oz. hot coffee
whipped cream

Stir coffee liqueur and tequila in a
coffee cup, add coffee, and top with
whipped cream.

Mimosa

3 oz. chilled champagne
3 oz. chilled orange juice

Pour orange juice into champagne flute
or wineglass, followed by champagne;
stir. The ratio of sparkling wine to juice
can be easily adjusted to fit one's tastes.

Mint Julep

4 sprigs mint
1 tsp. powdered sugar
2 tsp. water
2 ½ oz. bourbon

In a highball glass or silver julep cup, if
available, crush mint leaves, powdered
sugar, and water. Fill glass or mug with
shaved or crushed ice and add
bourbon. Top with more ice and
garnish with a mint sprig and straws.

Mojito

juice of ½ lime
½ tsp. powdered sugar
2 oz. white rum
soda
mint sprig

Stir sugar and lime juice well in a
highball glass. Crush mint leaves with a
pestle, add the squeezed half lime. Fill
with crushed ice, add rum, stir. Add
soda, and garnish with a mint sprig.

Moscow Mule

2 oz. vodka
iced ginger beer
juice of ½ lime

Pour vodka into a tall highball glass
with ice cubes or cracked ice. Squeeze
lime above drink and drop into glass.
Fill with ginger beer and stir.

Negroni

1 oz. gin
¾ oz. Campari
¾ oz. sweet vermouth
lemon

Stir with ice and strain into a cocktail
glass, or into an old-fashioned glass
over ice cubes. Add a twist of lemon
peel. A small amount of club soda is an
optional addition.

New Orleans Fizz

juice of ½ lemon
1 egg white
1 tsp. powdered sugar
dash fleurs d'orange (orange flower
    water)
¼ oz. cream
2 oz. gin
club soda

Shake first six ingredients well over ice
cubes in a shaker, strain into a collins
or highball glass filled with ice cubes,
and fill with soda.

New Yorker

1½ oz. bourbon
dashes grenadine
lime

Pour bourbon over ice cubes in an old-
fashioned glass, squeeze lime wedge
into drink and drop into glass, add
grenadine, stir well.

New York Flip

1 egg yolk
½ tsp. powdered sugar
¾ oz. cream
1 oz. bourbon
¾ oz. tawny port
nutmeg

Shake all but nutmeg well over ice
cubes in a shaker and strain into a
cocktail glass. Sprinkle top of drink
with nutmeg.

Old-Fashioned

1 sugar cube
1 dash bitters
1 tsp. water
2 oz. bourbon
lemon
orange
stemmed cherry

In an old-fashioned glass, combine
sugar cube, bitters, and water, and
muddle well. Add bourbon and stir.
Add a twist of lemon peel and ice
cubes. Decorate with slices of orange
and lemon, and a cherry.

Orange Fizz

2 oz. gin
1½ oz. orange juice
½ oz. lemon juice
2 tsp. triple sec
1 tsp. sugar
dashes orange bitters
club soda
orange

Combine all but soda with ice in a
shaker. Strain into a highball glass half-
filled with ice. Fill with soda and stir.
Garnish with orange slice.

Park Avenue

¼ oz. dry vermouth
¼ oz. sweet light vermouth
1 oz. gin
¼ oz. unsweetened pineapple juice

Stir well with ice in a mixing glass, and strain into a chilled cocktail glass.

Pimm's Cup

1¼–1¾ oz. Pimm's No. 1
7-Up
lemon
cucumber

Pour Pimm's over ice cubes into a large
highball glass, fill with 7-Up, add
lemon and cucumber peels. Pimm's
can also be prepared with ginger ale
(Pimm's Rangoon) or sparkling wine
(Pimm's Royal) in place of 7-Up.

Piña Colada

3 oz. light rum
3 tbsp. coconut milk
3 tbsp. crushed pineapple

Place ingredients in a blender with two
cups of crushed ice and blend at high
speed for a short time or mix in a
shaker with crushed ice. Strain into a
collins or highball glass and serve with
a straw. Pineapple juice can be
substituted for the crushed pineapple,
using equal parts rum and juice.

Pink Gin

3 dashes bitters
2 oz. gin

Pour the bitters into a wineglass. Swirl
the glass to coat the inside with the
bitters; shake out the excess. Pour the
gin into the glass. Do not add ice,
though ice water can be added if
desired. Also known as Gin & Bitters.

Pink Lady

2 oz. gin
1 tsp. grenadine
½ tsp. cherry brandy
½ oz. heavy cream
1 egg white

Combine all of the ingredients in a
shaker half-filled with ice cubes. Shake
well. Strain into a cocktail glass.

Pisco Sour

juice of ½ lemon
½–1 tsp. powdered sugar
1½ oz. Pisco brandy
stemmed cherry

Shake well over ice cubes in a shaker,
strain into a sour glass, and garnish
with a cherry.

Planter's Punch

juice of 2 limes
2 tsp. powdered sugar
2 oz. club soda
2 dashes bitters
2 ½ oz. light or dark rum
1 dash grenadine
lemon, orange, pineapple, stemmed
  cherry

Mix first three ingredients in a collins
glass, add ice cubes, and stir until glass
is frosted. Add bitters and rum. Stir
and top with grenadine. Decorate with
slices of lemon, orange, pineapple, and
a stemmed cherry. Serve with a straw.

Porto Flip

1 egg yolk
½ tsp. powdered sugar
¾ oz. cream
1½ oz. ruby port
¼ oz. brandy
nutmeg

Shake everything except nutmeg well
over ice in a shaker and strain into a
cocktail glass. Sprinkle top of drink
with nutmeg before serving.

Rob Roy

¾ oz. sweet vermouth
1½ oz. Scotch
stemmed cherry

Stir vermouth and Scotch with ice and
strain into a cocktail glass. Garnish
with a stemmed cherry. A dash of
Angostura bitters is an optional
addition. The Rob Roy is essentially a
Scotch Manhattan.

Rum Rickey

1½ oz. light rum
½ small lime
club soda

Add rum to a highball glass with ample
ice. Squeeze lime over the drink before
dropping it into the glass. Fill with
soda and stir.

Rum Sour

juice of ½ lemon
½–1 tsp. powdered sugar
2 oz. light rum
stemmed cherry

Shake with ice and strain into a sour or
cocktail glass. Decorate with a half-slice
of lemon and a cherry.

Rusty Nail

¾ oz. Scotch
¼ oz. Drambuie

Pour Scotch into an old-fashioned
glass with ice cubes. Float Drambuie
on top.

Rye Sour

juice of ½ lemon
½–1 tsp. powdered sugar
1½ oz. rye whiskey
stemmed cherry

Shake well over ice cubes in a shaker,
strain into a sour glass, and add cherry.

Salty Dog

1½ oz. vodka
3½ oz. grapefruit juice
salt

Shake with ice in a shaker and pour
into a chilled cocktail glass rimmed
with salt. A pinch of salt may also be
sprinkled into the drink. Gin may be
substituted for the vodka, using a
greater amount of juice, to taste.

Sazerac

½ teaspoon sugar
dash bitters (Peychaud's, if possible)
dash Pernod (or absinthe substitute)
2 oz. blended whiskey or bourbon
lemon
water or soda

Combine sugar, bitters, and 1 table-spoon of water in an old-fashioned glass and stir until sugar is dissolved. Add liquors and a large ice cube and stir well. Top with water or soda, and add lemon twist. For a slight variation coat the glass with Pernod to begin.

Scorpion

1½ oz. orange juice
¼ oz. triple sec
¾ oz. brandy
¾ oz. white rum
1 oz. dark rum
juice of ½ lime

Shake well over crushed ice, strain into
a large highball glass half-filled with
crushed ice, and drop the squeezed
lime into the glass before serving.

Scotch Martini

2½ oz. gin
dashes scotch
lemon

Strain iced gin into chilled cocktail
glass and add scotch. Garnish with
lemon peel.

Screwdriver

1 ½ oz. vodka
5 oz. orange juice

Pour vodka and juice into a highball
glass over ice cubes. Stir well.

Seabreeze

1½ oz. vodka
4 oz. cranberry juice
1 oz. grapefruit juice
lime

Pour into a highball glass over ice
cubes. Stir, and garnish with a wedge
of lime.

Shirley Temple

ginger ale
1 dash grenadine
orange
stemmed cherry

Add grenadine to a collins or highball
glass filled with ice; top with ginger ale.
Decorate with an orange slice and
cherry.

Sidecar

juice of ¼ lemon
1 oz. triple sec
1 oz. brandy

Shake all ingredients together with ice
and strain into a chilled cocktail glass.

Silver Bullet

1 oz. gin
1 oz. kümmel
1 tbsp. lemon juice

Shake all ingredients with ice and
strain into a cocktail glass.

Silver Fizz

juice of ½ lemon
1 egg white
1 tsp. powdered sugar
2 oz. gin
club soda

Shake first five ingredients well over ice
cubes in a shaker, strain into a collins
or highball glass over ice, and fill with
soda.

Singapore Sling

juice of ½ lemon
1 tsp. powdered sugar
2 oz. gin
club soda
½ oz. cherry-flavored brandy

Shake lemon, sugar, and gin with ice
and strain into a collins or highball
glass. Add ice cubes and fill with club
soda. Float cherry-flavored brandy on
top. Decorate with fruits in season and
serve with straws.

Southside

juice of ½ lemon
1 tsp. powdered sugar
1½ oz. gin
mint leaves

Crush a few mint leaves together with
lemon juice in a cocktail glass. Shake
gin and sugar with ice and strain into
the glass; stir well. Garnish with two
sprigs of fresh mint.

Strawberry Margarita

1½ oz. tequila
1 oz. lime juice
½ oz. triple sec
½ oz. strawberry schnapps or
    strawberry liqueur
lime

Shake all ingredients with ice and
strain into chilled cocktail glass.
Garnish with a lime wheel.

Tequila Sunrise

2 oz. tequila
4 oz. orange juice
¾ oz. grenadine
lime wedge

Squeeze lime into a large highball glass
half-filled with ice and drop it into the
glass. Stir tequila and orange juice with
ice and strain into the glass. Pour in
grenadine slowly and allow to settle.
Stir to complete the sunrise.

Tom Collins

juice of ½ lemon
1 tsp. powdered sugar
2 oz. gin
club soda
orange
lemon
stemmed cherry

Shake lemon juice, sugar, and gin with
ice and strain into a collins glass. Add
several ice cubes, fill with club soda,
and stir. Decorate with slices of lemon
and orange and a cherry. Serve with a
straw.

Vermouth Cocktail

1 oz. dry vermouth
1 oz. sweet light vermouth
1 dash orange bitters

Stir with ice and strain into a chilled
cocktail glass. Serve with a cherry. Also
known as a Half & Half.

Vodka Gimlet

1 oz. lime juice
1½ oz. vodka

Shake with ice and strain into a chilled
cocktail glass. Powdered sugar may also
be added, to taste. *See also* Gimlet.

"I never have more than one drink before dinner. But I do like that one to be large and very strong and very cold and very well-made."

—FROM *CASINO ROYALE*,
IAN FLEMING

Vodka Martini

2 ½ oz. vodka
1½ tsp. dry vermouth
1 lemon twist or 1 cocktail olive

In a mixing glass half-filled with ice cubes, combine the vodka and vermouth. Stir well. Strain into a chilled cocktail glass. Garnish with a lemon twist or an olive. *See also* Martini.

Vodka Sour

juice of ½ lemon
½–1 tsp. powdered sugar
1½ oz. vodka
stemmed cherry

Shake vodka, sugar syrup, and lemon
juice well over ice cubes in a shaker,
strain into a sour glass, and garnish
with a cherry.

Vodka Stinger

1 oz. vodka
1 oz. crème de menthe (white)

Shake with ice and strain into a small
highball glass with ice. Garnish with
mint, if desired.

"Try not to hold this
against me,
but I don't know what
a whiskey sour is."

—FROM *THIRTEEN DAYS*,
IAN JEFFERIES

Whiskey Mac

1½ oz. scotch
1 oz. ginger wine
lemon

Stir scotch and ginger wine with ice
in a shaker until cold, then strain into
a cocktail glass and garnish with
lemon peel.

Whiskey Sour

juice of ½ lemon
½–1 tsp. powdered sugar
1½ oz. blended whiskey
stemmed cherry

Shake with ice and strain into a chilled
sour or cocktail glass. Decorate with a
half-slice of lemon and a cherry.

White Russian

1 oz. coffee liqueur
2 oz. vodka
milk or cream

Pour coffee liqueur and vodka into an
old-fashioned glass over ice cubes and
fill with milk or cream. A White
Russian can also be served neat; simply
strain liquors into a cocktail glass and
top with milk or cream.

Zombie

1¼ oz. lemon juice
3 dashes grenadine
¾ oz. blood orange juice
¾ oz. cherry brandy
¾ oz. light rum
2 oz. dark rum
½ oz. high-proof dark rum

Combine all ingredients well over ice cubes in a shaker, and strain into a large, frosted highball glass over crushed ice. The drink can be garnished with a stick of pineapple, a cherry, or a sprig of fresh mint dipped in powdered sugar.

Cocktail
Chronology

Cocktail Chronology

7TH CENTURY B.C.
Greek symposium (and social drinking) initiated.

478 B.C.
Confucius warns against drunkenness.

14TH CENTURY A.D.
First mixed drink, the Bragget, concocted by combining mead and ale.

1720
So-called Gin Epidemic begins in London.

1736
Britain passes the Gin Act to limit gin production.

1742
Gin Act repealed.

22 MARCH 1773
Chemist Joseph Priestly invents carbonated water.

1784
Benjamin Rush, "father of the temperance move-

ment," publishes *An Inquiry into the Effects of Ardent Spirits upon the Human Minde and Body*.

13 MAY 1806
First known use in print of the word "cocktail," attributed to the American periodical *The Balance*.

1 MAY 1851
Opening of the first cocktail bar, at Gore House near Hyde Park, London.

4 OCTOBER 1851
First cocktail bar closes. License not renewed.

1860
"First" Martini served by infamous barman "Professor" Jerry Thomas, at the Occidental Hotel, San Francisco. See "The Martini: A Brief History" following chronology.

1862
Jerry Thomas publishes first cocktail book,

The Bar-Tender's Guide (also known as *The Bon Vivant's Guide, or How to Mix Drinks*).

1874
Another "first" Martini served by Julio Richelieu in Martinez, California.

16 DECEMBER 1899
Birth of Noel Coward: "For gin, in cruel/Sober truth,/Supplies the fuel/For flaming youth."

1915
Singapore Sling created at Raffles Hotel bar by legendary bartender Ngiam Tong Boon to suit the tastes of visitors from the West.

17 JUNE 1917
Birth of Dean Martin (Dino Paul Crocetti): "I feel sorry for people who don't drink. Every morning they must get up knowing they won't feel any better all day."

16 JANUARY 1920
Prohibition becomes law in the United States.

FRANK   SINATRA
DEAN   MARTIN
SAMMY   DAVIS JR.
PETER   LAWFORD
JOEY   BISHOP

IN THE LOUNGE
JONAH JONES
NORMAN BRO
BROOK

1920
Bloody Mary (then called Bucket of Blood) invented by bartender Fernand L. Petiot at Harry's New York Bar in Paris.

26 APRIL 1924
British writer Alec Waugh (brother of author Evelyn) throws "first" cocktail party.

5 DECEMBER 1933
Prohibition repealed.

12 MAY 1935
Alcoholics Anonymous founded by William Wilson ("Bill W").

1939
So-called Cocktail Age ends. Germany invades Poland.

1944
The Mai Tai invented in Oakland by Californian Victor "Trader Vic" Bergeron, who also concocts

the Fog Cutter, Scorpion, and others.

1945
The Lost Weekend is released.

22 AUGUST 1949
T. S. Eliot's play *The Cocktail Party* opens at Edinburgh Festival, starring Alec Guiness.

1953
James Bond offers up his own recipe for the Vodka Martini in Ian Fleming's first Bond book, *Casino Royale*.

OCTOBER 1996
Swingers, a hit independent film celebrating lounge culture, is released. Cocktail age reborn.

The Martini: A Brief History

*I*t would be heresy to question the Martini's place in the cocktail realm. Still, the monarch of the mixed drink has a history as murky as the drink is clean and clear.

In *Stirred—Not Shaken*, John Doxat's paean to the Martini, he traces the drink to around 1910, when it was invented for John D. Rockefeller by a bartender named Martini at New York's Knickerbocker Hotel.

In Martinez, California, however, a bronze plaque states that this rather innocuous county seat some twenty miles from San Francisco is the birthplace of the Martini. "On this site in 1874," reads the sign, "Julio Richelieu, bartender, served up the first Martini when a miner came into his saloon . . . and asked for something special. He was served a 'Martinez Special.' After three or four drinks, however, the 'z' would get very much in the way."

The earliest incarnation of the Martini, however, has been linked to the godfather of the modern cocktail, "Professor" Jerry Thomas (also credited with writing

the first authoritative bartender's guide). According to the story, Thomas set up a bar in the Occidental Hotel on San Francisco's Montgomery Street around 1860. Someone on his way to Martinez stopped in and requested something special. "Very well," Thomas allegedly replied, "here is a new drink I have invented for your trip. We'll call it the Martinez."

Anyone who has spent any time in bars has no doubt overheard some tale about the Martini. In New York, I was once told that the drink was named after the Martini sisters, who were Roaring Twenties entertainers of some sort. Martini and Rossi dry vermouth has been said (by no less than the *Oxford English Dictionary*) to be the namesake, although it seems the cocktail was around in America long before that brand was.

None of the early recipes much remind one of the modern-day Martini, except that gin was an ingredient. (Charles Schumann writes in *American Bar*, however, that gin as we know it today was only produced around the beginning of the century.) The drink has long been tinkered with: add cocktail onions instead of olives (or a twist) and you have a Gibson. Recently a New York bar received special mention for a Martini that had gourmet black olives and a dash of fine balsamic vinegar.

The biggest challenge to purists, of course, is the current popularity of the Vodka Martini, or Vodkatini, as Europeans call it. As Kathlyn and Martin Gay point out in their encyclopedia of drinking and eating customs, "Some traditional Martini drinkers have switched to vodka. . . . However, the rest of the ritual— from the amount of the vermouth used to the way the drink is served—remains fairly consistent."

The Martini also owns the distinction of having the best quote associated with it: "I must get out of these wet clothes and into a dry Martini." Naturally, it is attributed to various celebrities, including Mae West, Robert Benchley, and Alexander Woollcott.

Glassware
& Bar
Equipment

Glassware

The long and short of glassware is: size matters. Have a variety of sizes. Do not worry too much about the styling of glasses, with one exception—the Martini glass.

CHAMPAGE FLUTE: A bit specialized perhaps, but designed with those bubbles in mind.

MARTINI GLASS: The classic design; both a circle and a triangle. Minimalist and deceptively capacious. Barnaby Conrad III writes: "It is as poised as a ballerina on point and its contents must be imbibed with care." Suitable for nearly any mixed drink served neat—that, is without ice. The cocktail glass is a relation to the Martini glass; it features a rounded cup instead of the Martini's triangle.

HIGHBALL, OR COLLINS GLASS: A large, multi-purpose cocktail glass. For everything from a Gin Fizz to a Long Island Iced Tea. Holds between eight and twelve ounces.

OLD-FASHIONED GLASS: The stout, sturdy tumbler. Perfect for a Manhattan on the rocks. Fine for a Caipirinha. Standard issue for B & B. Contains between six and ten ounces.

SOUR GLASS: A narrow, stemmed glass perfectly proportioned for sours of four to seven ounces.

WINEGLASS: Useful for cream drinks and punches, and in a pinch can fill in for just about any drink.

That is the basic lineup. Of course, many more could be on hand for specialty drinks. Common sense dictates that if you are going to serve a hot drink, it should be poured into a glass that will not break from the heat.

Bar Equipment

The list of "necessary" equipment and glassware in most bartender's guides is nearly enough to put one off the notion of mixing drinks. Here, however, are some key components to have behind the bar:

CAN OPENER.

JIGGER: The best one is two-sided: the larger cup holds either two ounces or one and a half ounces; the smaller side holds either one ounce or three quarters of an ounce.

JUICER: The difference between fresh-squeezed juice and store-bought varieties can be enormous— maybe not with a Screwdriver, but certainly with a Margarita. An old-fashioned juicer with a bowl is sufficient.

LONG SPOON, OR STIRRER: Let's face it, anything that is clean and can reach the bottom of the mixing glass will suffice.

PARING KNIFE AND CUTTING BOARD: Neither need be elaborate. A sharp blade is essential. The board does not have to be large; you will be most often cutting lime wedges or trimming peels for a twist.

SHAKER: *The* fundamental item. It should be large enough to handle two full drinks and ice, approximately 14 ounces. The Boston shaker is a popular model. It pairs one tall glass with a slightly larger steel container. Another favorite shaker is the stainless steel variety that comes with a strainer built into the lid and a cap roughly the size of a two-ounce jigger. This style of shaker conveniently eliminates two pieces of equipment generally considered required: the strainer and the jigger/shot glass.

STRAINER: A piece of ice ruins a neat drink. If you opt for a shaker that cannot perform the task of straining, get a Hawthorn strainer, the type with

the coil spring around its head to keep it snug. It is functional and has a certain amount of retro-chic.

WAITER'S CORKSCREW: Ideal because it folds up like a pocket knife and includes a standard bottle opener, too.

Glossary

Glossary

ANGOSTURA BITTERS: Best-selling brand of bitters, named after a town in Venezuela where a physician from Germany made it to combat malaria. Consists of an extract from the bark of the Casparia tree, plus herbs and spices.

APERITIF: From the Latin word *aperire,* to open. Starter or before-dinner drink.

BÉNÉDICTINE: a light green aromatic cordial, formerly made by monks of the Bénédictine order in Normandy.

CASSIS, CRÈME DE CASSIS: Black currant cordial.

CHASER: Nonalcoholic (usually) liquid such as water or soda used to follow a stiff (usually) drink.

COINTREAU: White French liqueur flavored with the peel of curaçao and other oranges.

COLLINS: Of the Collinses, the Tom Collins is most common. In general, the word describes a drink made with liquor, sugar (or more successfully, sugar syrup), lemon juice, and club soda; stirred not shaken, garnished with cherry and orange slice. (To make 16 ounces of sugar syrup, slowly dissolve a pound of granulated sugar in 13 ounces of hot water.)

CURAÇAO: Orange-flavored liqueur originally produced in Holland from sour oranges, cane sugar, and brandy.

DRAMBUIE: Liqueur made from Scotch whisky, honey, herbs, and spices.

DIGESTIF: After-dinner drink; also known as a nightcap.

JIGGER: A small measuring cup generally equal to one and a half ounces.

FIFTH: Seven hundred fifty milliliters, or approximately 25.4 ounces; about a fifth of a gallon.

FIZZ: Drink with carbonated water that is shaken before serving, ideally with the glass foaming at the brim.

FLIP: Drink with egg yolk and sugar that is shaken before serving. Related to the egg nog, though lacking cream or milk.

FLOAT: A minute portion of liquor poured gently on top of a drink.

HIGHBALL: Any tall drink over ice with plain or carbonated waters, always without juice.

JULEP: A drink consisting of spirits with mint and sugar syrup.

NEAT: Describes a drink served without ice.

ROSE'S LIME JUICE: Best-known brand, which allegedly predates the drink most closely associated with it: the Gimlet. First made by Lauchlin Rose of

Scotland in 1867, sold to shipping companies to relieve scurvy among sailors.

SLING: Mix of lemon and sugar or sweet liqueur.

SOUR: A drink of liquor, lemon juice, and sugar (and sometimes a bit of orange juice, too).

TRIPLE SEC: A liqueur made from citrus fruits; Cointreau is the best-known variety of triple sec.

TWIST: A small slice of citrus peel, squeezed over a drink (and, on occasion, rubbed around the rim of the glass).

VERMOUTH: A French appetizer wine, dry (white) or sweet (white or red), flavored with up to fifty herbs, roots, berries, and even flowers. More commonly used as a mixer than as a cordial.

Selected Bibliography

Babor, Thomas, Ph.D. *Alcohol: Customs and Rituals*. New York: Chelsea House, 1986.
A volume of the *Encyclopedia of Psychoactive Drugs*. Histories and comparative studies of drinking in different countries.

Barr, Andrew. *Drink*. New York: Bantam, 1995.
An enthusiastic look at historic and contemporary consumption of alcohol in Great Britain, for the most part.

Conrad, Barnaby, III. *The Martini*. San Francisco: Chronicle Books, 1995.
A coffee table book replete with myth and lore. Dozens of illustrations, including views of the Martini as seen by artists such as Mondrian, Oldenburg, and Ruscha.

Cotton, Leo, edited by Susan Suffes. *Mr. Boston: Official Bartender's and Party Guide*. New York: Warner Books, 1994.
The old bible of cocktails. Authoritative, given its more than sixty editions since 1935. Complete with bar tricks.

Dunkling, Leslie. *The Guinness Drinking Companion*. London: Guinness Publishing, 1992.

Surprisingly nonregional and an excellent
source of literary references to drink.

Gay, Kathlyn, and Martin Gay. *Encyclopedia of
North American Eating & Drinking Traditions,
Customs & Rituals*. Santa Barbara, Calif.:
ABC-Clio, 1996.
More about eating than drinking.

Jackson, Michael. *Michael Jackson's Cocktail Book*.
London: Mitchell Beazley, 1994.
Well-illustrated book from the author of the
better-known *World Guide to Whisky* and
Pocket Bartender's Guide.

Regan, Gary. *The Bartender's Bible*. New York:
HarperCollins, 1991.
One thousand and one mixed drinks in a
handy, lie-flat, spiral-bound book.

Schumann, Charles. *American Bar*. New York:
Abbeville Press, 1995.
The new bible of cocktails. Handsome, infor-
mative, if surprisingly sober.

Indices

Drink Name Index

Ingredient Index

Drink Type Index

Acknowledgments

The publisher wishes to thank the following New York bars and restaurants for their expertise and for graciously allowing photographers to shoot on their premises (numerals refer to pages on which those sites appear):

City Wine & Cigar Co. (34, 56, 152, 170)
Fez (65, 66, 164)
Flamingo East (160, 184, 186)
Global 33 (143, 156)
Gramercy Tavern (105, 123, 228)
Harry Cipriani (29, 82, 149, 174)
Indochine (159, 168)
King Cole Room at the St. Regis (2, 37, 55, 231)
Monkey Bar (20, 61, 267)
Pravda (34, 110)
River Cafe (front cover, 6, 176, 192)

Photography Credits

Front cover: Rum Sour. See page 177.

Back cover: Zombie. See page 233.

Spine: Manhattan. See page 121.

Fronispiece: Champagne Cocktail. See page 54.

Page 9: Frank Sinatra and Grace Kelly, *High Society*, 1956.

Page 40: Lars Hanson, Greta Garbo, and John Gilbert, *Flesh and the Devil*, 1927.

Page 78: Humphrey Bogart and Ingrid Bergman, *Casablanca*, 1942.

Page 100: George Peppard and Audrey Hepburn, *Breakfast at Tiffany's*, 1961.

Page 124: Frank Sinatra and Bing Crosby, *High Society*, 1956.

Page 128: Dick Powell, Barry Sullivan, and Lana Turner, *The Bad and the Beautiful*, 1952.

Page 216: Sean Connery and Mai Ling, *Goldfinger*, 1964.

Page 224: Audrey Hepburn and George Peppard, *Breakfast at Tiffany's*, 1961.

Page 239: Frank Sinatra, Dean Martin, Sammy Davis Jr., Peter Lawford, and Joey Bishop outside the Sands Hotel, Las Vegas, c. 1960.

Page 243: Bernard Lee and Sean Connery, *Goldfinger*, 1964.

Page 286: Tom Cruise, *Cocktail*, 1988.

Editor: Jeffrey Golick
Art Director: Patricia Fabricant
Designer: Molly Shields
Typesetter: Laura Lindgren
Picture Editor: Naomi Ben-Shahar
Picture Researcher: Scott Hall
Production Manager: Vicki Russell

First edition
10 9 8

Library of Congress Cataloging-in-Publication Data
Shelby, Barry.
　　100 classic cocktails / by Barry Shelby.
　　　　p.　　cm.
　　Includes bibliographical references and index.
　　ISBN 0-7892-0426-6
　　1. Cocktails.　I. Title.　II. Title : one hundred classic cocktails
TX951.S54　1998
641.8'74—dc21　　　　　　　　　　　　　　　　97-38699

About the Author

Barry Shelby spent some thirteen years trolling the bars in and around New York City, where he worked as an editor for *World Press Review* magazine. He also developed a reputation for mixing a mean, desert-dry Martini on request. He now lives in Scotland.

Selected List of Tiny Folios™ from Abbeville Press

- Angels • 0-7892-0403-7 • $11.95

- Ansel Adams: The National Park Service Photographs
  1-55859-817-0 • $11.95

- Art of Rock: Posters from Presley to Punk
  1-55859-606-2 • $11.95

- The Great Book of French Impressionism
  0-7892-0405-3 • $11.95

- Hot Rods and Cool Customs • 0-7892-0026-0 • $11.95

- Hugs & Kisses • 0-7892-0361-8 • $11.95

- The Life of Christ • 0-7892-0144-5 • $11.95

- Minerals and Gems from the American Museum
  of Natural History • 1-55859-273-3 • $11.95

- Norman Rockwell: 332 Magazine Covers
  0-7892-0409-6 • $11.95

- Rock and Royalty, by Gianni Versace • 0-7892-0489-4 • $11.95

- Treasures of the Louvre • 0-7892-0406-1 • $11.95

- Yellowstone: National Park • 1-55859-825-1 • $11.95